Introduction

I grew up in Kesgrave on the outskirts of Ipswich in Suffolk during the 1960s and 1970s, becoming interested in buses in 1976 after my first ride on a Bristol Lodekka.

After leaving school in 1978 I worked for a local family office equipment company, G. E. Woodward, based in Princes Street, Ipswich, and from there I made the decision in 1986 to move to London to work as a bus driver, passing through London Transport's Chiswick training school later that same year. I've driven many types of bus in service, not just in London, but also when I worked as a bus driver in Stevenage and also First Eastern Counties in Ipswich.

I've been back in London now for the past eleven years, driving buses in the Enfield area. But the enthusiast in me still misses the wonderful era of the seventies and eighties, of the National Bus Company and the buses of that time.

The English Bus Scene Since 1990 is a photographic journey through my places of work, as well as holidays and days out around England, with a little help from fellow author Robert Appleton, who has kindly provided twenty images from areas that I have not visited.

Deregulation of the bus industry happened in 1986, and prior to this some of the larger operators within the National Bus Company, like Bristol Omnibus and Eastern Counties, were split to provide two smaller operators instead of one. Initially this created a wide variety of operators and liveries, some of which are seen in this book, though many liveries are now just a memory of yet another era that has passed. Over a period of time the industry has developed in such a way that we have some large groups, such as Arriva, First, Go-Ahead and Stagecoach, which dominate, with plenty of room for independent operators to continue to add variety. But even these large groups are cutting back, and lack of government funding is fuelling a steady decline in rural bus services.

Although London has avoided deregulation, London Transport started placing bus routes in the capital out for competitive tender in 1985, and a wide variety of operators and liveries could be seen far and wide across the capital. The privatisation of London Buses came in 1994, and further down the line Transport for London's policy of initially an 80 per cent red livery, and later a 100 per cent red livery, has taken away much of the interest and variety surrounding the bus scene in the capital.

The photographs in this book are in no particular order, but I hope that you will enjoy this photographic journey from 1990 up to the present.

Finally, the following sources of information have been invaluable in providing information for the captions that accompany my photographs:

Bus Lists on the Web: http://www.buslistsontheweb.co.uk/.
Flickr: https://www.flickr.com/.
PSV Circle News-Sheets.
Bus Handbooks (British Bus Publishing).
25 Years of Yorkshire Coastliner by Christopher Clarkson (Buyrightprint).

Additional thanks to Robert Appleton, who has kindly supplied some images from areas I have not visited.

THE ENGLISH BUS SCENE SINCE 1990

Peter Horrex

AMBERLEY

First published 2018

Amberley Publishing
The Hill, Stroud
Gloucestershire, GL5 4EP

www.amberley-books.com

Copyright © Peter Horrex, 2018

The right of Peter Horrex to be identified as
the Author of this work has been asserted in
accordance with the Copyrights, Designs and
Patents Act 1988.

ISBN 978 1 4456 7783 5 (print)
ISBN 978 1 4456 7784 2 (ebook)

British Library Cataloguing in Publication Data.
A catalogue record for this book is available from
the British Library.

Origination by Amberley Publishing.
Printed in the UK.

The year is 1990, and the bus scene across England is offering a whole host of varied liveries and operators as deregulation of the bus industry is in full swing – except for London, though even here things have been changing since the mid-1980s, with new operators bringing their own liveries to the streets of London, having successfully tendered for routes and taken them away from London Buses. Kentish Bus Northern Counties-bodied Leyland Olympian G544 VBB collects passengers in New Oxford Street. Kentish Bus took over operation of the 55 on 24 February 1990 from a base in Leyton, and this bus was new for that contract.

Routemaster buses, of course, were still common on the streets of London back in 1990. RM1392 (392 CLT) heads along Oxford Street towards her terminus at Bloomsbury on route 7. By now London Buses had been divided into twelve operating units in preparation for privatisation, and route 7 was being operated by CentreWest, an operating subsidiary of London Buses.

Ipswich Buses were to operate a number of Dennis Falcons throughout the late 1980s and into the twenty-first century, including some second-hand examples. In my opinion these Northern Counties-bodied examples were more attractive than their East Lancs-bodied counterparts. C107S DX was new to Ipswich Buses in February 1986 and is seen here in Tower Ramparts bus station in 1990.

In order for London Buses to effectively compete with outside operators for London work, second-hand buses were acquired during 1987 from both Yorkshire and West Midlands PTE. These were divided between Potters Bar and Harrow Weald garages. The Potters Bar examples were common on, among others, route W8, which was known as a 'block grant' route – in other words, a route that had not yet been placed out for tender and was still operated by London Buses. JOV 778P had been new to West Midlands PTE in April 1976, and is seen here during the summer of 1990, bound for Lower Edmonton.

Arriving in to London Buses stock in November 1984 were a batch of three Northern Counties-bodied Dennis Dominators, which were part of the Alternative Vehicle Evaluation trials that were being undertaken by London Buses at the time. These smart buses were initially based at Stockwell garage and they remained unique in the London Buses fleet. H2 (B102 WUW) is seen awaiting departure time while working route 133, bound for Elephant and Castle.

The Leyland Titan would provide sterling service for London in to the twenty-first century, with over a thousand examples being purchased by London Transport. T981 (A981 SYE) was delivered new in April 1984, and is pictured here in Clapham in 1990 working for the London Buses subsidiary London Central, on route 35.

Nelson Independent Bus Services were operating Bristol RE TUO 259J when she was photographed here arriving in Basildon in 1990. This bus had been new to Western National in January 1971, and she came to NIBS from Southern National. She was scrapped in late 1994.

DMS 2404 (OJD 404R) was new to London Transport in May 1977. Operating for London General, she is seen here passing along Whitehall on route 88 in 1990. The history of route 88 can be traced back as far as 1934, and peak hour operation required fifty-three buses. By 1990 the route had been shortened and the peak hour weekday operation called for twenty-seven Routemaster buses, with twenty being required on a Saturday. Sundays were driver-only operation and called for eighteen buses, a mixture of Metrobuses and Fleetlines.

Although the history of London bus route 125 can be traced back as far as 1937, the route settled into its present form without any weekend variations in February 1992, running between Finchley Central station and Winchmore Hill. Grey-Green 119 (F119 PHM), an Alexander-bodied Volvo Citybus new in 1988, is seen passing through Southgate in 1991.

Leyland Atlantean MVK 506R was new to Tyne & Wear PTE in December 1976 carrying Alexander AL type H48/31D bodywork, and was initially given fleet number 506. In this 1991 view she is seen passing through South Shields as part of the Busways fleet. She was later acquired by Strathclyde Buses and by 1993 had moved in to that operator's low-cost unit, GCT.

Badgerlines GHY 138K is a dual-purpose Bristol RELH that was new in August 1972 to the Bristol Omnibus Company. Pictured here in 1991 leaving Wells bound for Weston-super-Mare on route 126, she was sold on to Northern Bus in January 1992, before being scrapped three years later in January 1995.

New to Trimdon Motor Services in April 1981, LPY 460W is a Leyland Leopard that originally carried Duple Dominant B55F bodywork before being re-bodied in 1995 by East Lancs. She is seen here working for United, passing through Stockton-on-Tees in 1991.

Leyland Olympian B268 LPH was new to London Country in May 1985. In this 1991 view she is pictured in the bus station in Keighley while working for Keighley & District, before she returned south a few years later within the Blazefield group to work for Sovereign Bus & Coach, and then Huntingdon & District.

With a variety of operators and liveries on the scene in London, there were also a mix of both new and second-hand vehicles. EWF 451V is a Metrobus that was originally new to South Yorkshire PTE in January 1980, and is seen here in 1991 working for Grey-Green at Cockfosters in 1991 on London Regional Transport route 298.

In October 1990 Thamesway took delivery of Leyland Olympian H104 KVX as part of a batch of four acquired for use on newly awarded London route 307. Thamesway was Eastern National's unit formed to operate the tendered London services out of Walthamstow and Ponders End. In this 1991 view H104 KVX, given fleet number 1004, collects passengers on the border of Cockfosters and Southgate.

Bristol RELL OWC 720M was new to Colchester Corporation Transport in December 1973. She saw further service with Busways Travel Services before being withdrawn in 1998, after which she entered preservation. She is seen here passing through South Shields in the summer of 1991.

There was no such thing as a kneeling, low-floor bus back in 1991, and passengers here are managing to board away from the kerb without much fuss. Leyland Leopard 311 (WCW 311R) was new in April 1977 to Lancaster City Transport, carrying a rather nice style of bodywork by Alexander. She is seen here collecting passengers in Morecambe.

London's so-called 'New Routemaster' or Borisbus has received a mixed reaction from enthusiasts, who are fairly evenly split between liking and disliking the type. Personally I feel the rear end styling is more pleasing on the eye than the front end. Go-Ahead's LT501 (LTZ 1501) illustrates the rear end while passing through Vauxhall on 11 March 2016.

Tiger Line's T5 service operated between Amersham and Hatfield back in 2010. Posing for the camera at Hatfield on 18 November 2010 is UXI 1376, a Leyland Tiger that was new to Ulsterbus in March 1992, carrying Alexander (Belfast) Q type bodywork.

Carters Coach Services, originally associated more with operations in the Colchester and north Essex areas, were by now based in Capel St Mary in Suffolk with more work locally to the Ipswich area. On 3 November 2005 Carters K418 MGN pauses at Thorington Street, working back to Hadleigh from Colchester on their long-established route 755. This Plaxton-bodied Dennis Dart was new to R&I Tours in March 1993, but had also worked in London for Metroline.

New in August 1990 to Badgerline, Leyland Lynx H616 YTC passes through Radstock in 1992, working service 173 to Bath.

Trustybus, part of Galleon Travel, had previously operated as Trustline before selling out to Centrebus. Their nice bright livery can be seen to good effect here as Dennis Trident LK03 GFX leaves Waltham Cross bus station in June 2014 to terminate at the rail station. This bus was new to Metroline as TP 431 in June 2003.

Starting life with London Buses in July 1990, Carlyle-bodied Dennis Dart G39 TGW was photographed in Bognor Regis on 27 October 2010 while working for Emsworth & District, a company that has been providing bus and coach services in West Sussex and Hampshire since 1977.

Plaxton-bodied Volvo B6 M592 ANG is seen here in Brundish in Suffolk in the summer of 2001, working one of my favourite routes to drive, the 82 between Ipswich and Diss, taking in some lovely Suffolk countryside. This bus came to Eastern Counties after a failed attempt by Sheffield Mainline to operate over some bus routes in Ipswich.

New to London Country in June 1982, Roe-bodied Leyland Olympian TPD 120X was working for London & Country when photographed in Kingston upon Thames in 1993 while on London Transport service 57.

Back in 2012 and into 2013 I was working for TWH (Travel with Hunny), and one route operated around Dagenham was the MB1 Mecca Bingo contract. Over time, a variety of vehicles were operated on this route, but on the occasion of 20 December 2012 Optare Spectra YCZ 101 was on loan.

Ipswich Buses had a number of Dennis Falcons in their fleet, with a mix of bodywork shared between Northern Counties and East Lancs. I by far preferred the look of those with Northern Counties bodies, as seen in this view of C109 SDX passing through the town centre in 1994.

2 February 2009 and no buses operated all day from Metrolines Potters Bar garage; indeed, across London services were patchy all day. A mixture of Dennis Darts, Enviro 200s and Dennis Tridents shiver in the freezing temperatures.

In February 1976 Eastern Counties took delivery of Bristol VR 166 MCL 942P. Twenty years later, in the summer of 1996, she was photographed in Cambridge while working for Cambus, having moved to this operator in September 1984. Cambus was formed out of the split of Eastern Counties.

Logic Bus provided some local services around Cheshunt and Waltham Cross back in 2012. Logic Bus 130 (V130 GBY) is an ex-Metroline Dennis Dart that was new in 1999, and is seen here at Hammond Street on 29 March 2012.

At Kingston upon Thames in 1993 is this Wright Handybus Dennis Dart, JDZ 2409, seen working for Westlink on a London Regional Transport tendered service. New to London Buses in December 1990, these small buses were actually rather nice to drive, albeit a bit cramped in the driver's cab.

This Marshall-bodied Dennis Dart, P831 BUD, had been new in March 1997 to Forrest of Bootle. She was photographed in Harlow in Essex on 13 October 2010 while working for S. M. Coaches, a family run company that had links with Roadrunner and Olympian Coaches in the same town.

Back in 1993 The Bee Line Leyland National NRD 136M and Bristol VR WJM 821T pass each other in the town centre of Slough. It's not surprising that both of these vehicles had been new to Alder Valley, given that The Bee Line was formed out of part of that company following deregulation.

Basingstoke in Hampshire is the route being worked by Plaxton-bodied Dennis Dart X971 VAP, working for Stagecoach on 31 March 2012, having been delivered new in October 2000 to Sussex Coastline.

A lovely sunny day and Eastern Counties Leyland Olympian G133 ATW waits at Shotley in Suffolk on 29 April 2005. This bus had been new in 1989 to Ensign of Purfleet and was bodied by Northern Counties.

New to Badgerline in October 1989, Leyland Olympian G902 TWS pulls out of the bus station in Bath in 1991, working service 339 to Bristol. Note the odd destination arrangements, with a traditional scroll blind along with a dot matrix for the route number.

The Imperial Bus Company have been a familiar sight around north-east London for a number of years. Back in December 2009 their H1 service between Harlow and Loughton was about to be withdrawn, and Dennis Dart N261 PJR stands at Loughton station on 16 December 2009 before heading back to Harlow. This bus had been new to Hylton Castle of East Boldon in November 1995.

Great Yarmouth Transport operated a number of Bristol VRs in their fleet, of which RVF 36R is an example. Seen passing through the town centre of its home town in 1997, now some twenty years old, she had been new to this operator back in February 1977. By the time this photograph was taken Great Yarmouth Transport was part of First Eastern Counties and trading as First Blue Bus. RVF 36R was withdrawn and scrapped in the summer of 1997.

By the end of 2017, Arriva's aging VLA class of Volvo B7Tls were still soldiering on in North London. Here VLA2 (LJ03 MYR) heads away from Turnpike Lane bus station on 26 July 2017, having been new to Arriva London South in 2003.

Northern Counties-bodied Dennis Dominator H266 KVX was new in January 1991 to Frontrunner SE of Dagenham. The following year she was photographed leaving the bus station in Walthamstow with Capital Citybus, working London Transport service 97, bound for Chingford.

One of the most enjoyable bus driving jobs I've had was working for Travel with Hunny, known as TWH. Acquired late in 2013 for use on a new school service that required a high-capacity double-decker, TWH L392 LNA is seen at Bumbles Green on 4 September 2013 while working stage service 555 between Waltham Abbey and Harlow. This bus is a Dennis Dragon that was originally purchased by Stagecoach for use in their Kenya operations, but that was imported to the UK a few years later.

In 2007 the Blazefield Holdings operations in Lancashire and Yorkshire were sold to Transdev Group. Investment in new buses continued, as shown by Yorkshire Coastliner 424 (BD11 CEK) at Malton bus station and depot on 29 June 2017. She was one of a batch of four Volvo B9TL with Wrightbus Eclipse Gemini bodies and seventy semi-coach seats new in April 2011. Note the Yorkshire Coastliner route map on the offside staircase panels. (Robert Appleton)

The Metrobus provided sterling service to the travelling public of London. The type was first introduced to the capital in April 1978, with some example still remaining in service some twenty-four years later. By 2008, when this photograph was taken, the type was restricted to a few driver training buses. This is Arriva's C405 BUV, seen passing through Edmonton Green on 6 May 2008.

The Bendybus in London had an unfortunate history, plagued early on by a series of fires and being too easy for passengers to have a free ride by boarding any of the three large entrances/exits. Too large for much of London, the type was withdrawn prematurely. Depicting the type here is Arriva London North's BX04 NDK, seen arriving at Edmonton Green at the end of her journey on route 149 on 16 July 2007.

New in 2004, Stagecoach's Plaxton-bodied Dennis Dart GX04 EYB passes through Chichester on 27 October 2007, bound for East Wittering on route 53.

I enjoyed my time working for First Eastern Counties, and particularly loved driving their Scania L113 and L94 buses. Depicting the latter type, Wright-bodied W599 SNG was part of a batch purchased in May 2000 for Superoute 66, but is seen here at Shotley in 2001.

Stagecoach Manchester 12209 (MX13 FLV) is an Alexander Dennis E40H Enviro 400 with a diesel-electric hybrid drive system. She is 10.9 metres long with seventy-eight seats. Photographed in London Road, Manchester, on 9 April 2013, she is seen working service 192 from Manchester to Stockport, which continues beyond Stockport to Hazel Grove or Stepping Hill Hospital. (Robert Appleton)

New to Western SMT in December 1977, Alexander-bodied Leyland Leopard TSJ 64S was working for Rallybeam of Debach when photographed at Farlingaye School in Woodbridge, Suffolk, on a school service in 2000, still wearing London Links livery from her previous owner.

KDB 127V was a Leyland Fleetline with a Gardner 6LXB engine and Northern Counties seventy-five-seat body, and was new to Greater Manchester Transport in 1980. Subsequently, she saw service with Greater Manchester Buses, then Greater Manchester Buses North, which was purchased by First Group. KDB 127V was transferred to First Calderline and numbered 7256 in that fleet, and is seen leaving Halifax bus station on 12 February 1999. (Robert Appleton)

Eastern Counties P548 RNG, a Wright-bodied Scania L133, is photographed here at Ipswich on 29 April 2005. This was part of a batch acquired in June 1997 for use on the Superoute 88 group of services between Ipswich, Stowmarket and Bury St Edmunds, and she still carries part of the route branding above the windows.

These lovely Enviro 200 MMC BYD electric buses are in use by Go-Ahead's London General company on the 'Red Arrow' services out of their depot at Waterloo. Here Go-Ahead SEe47 (LJ66 CJO) arrives at Victoria on 20 August 2017.

RM1650 (650 DYE) was new to London Transport back in July 1963, and was one of a number of vehicles chosen for this livery for HRH Queen Elizabeth's Golden Jubilee back in 2002. She is seen here working for First London in 2002, passing along Oxford Street on route 23.

Safeguard of Guildford purchased Plaxton-bodied Dennis Dart K628 YPL new back in June 1993. Nine years later she was photographed passing through her home town while working local service 5.

In May 1996, Essex Buses, which included both Thamesway and Eastern National, purchased Dennis Dart N976 EHJ for use on their London operations. She is seen here when just a few months old, heading out of Enfield towards Edmonton Green on London Transport tendered service 191.

New to the Western National Omnibus Company in August 1978, this ECW-bodied Bristol VR, XDV 607S, had passed to Cambus in 1986, where she remained for ten years. Passing to Towler of Emneth in January 1997, she was subsequently scrapped in 2004. In this 1996 view she is seen departing the Drummer Street bus station in Cambridge.

The use of coaches on normal stage carriage work was common back in the days of the National Bus Company, and this continued in to the early years of deregulation. Leyland Leopard DAK 221V, part of United Auto's fleet, was photographed in 1991 at Barnard Castle.

Adding much-needed variety to the London bus scene is Metroline's electric bus BYD 1473 (LJ16 EZO). Seen at Marble Arch on 27 August 2017, this bus was new in March 2016.

Olympian Coaches V196 ERG is seen at St Margarets on 10 March 2013, working Sunday service C3 from Harlow to Waltham Cross, although through passengers had to change at Hoddesdon. This Dennis Dart SLF was new to Go Wear Buses in January 2000.

New to the Borough of Ipswich in March 1977, Roe-bodied Leyland Atlantean SDX 22R was still working for Ipswich Buses when photographed in the town in 1993.

Routemaster buses can still be seen on the streets of London, but are limited to heritage route 15, a short working that overlaps the standard 15 service, as depicted by Stagecoach RM2089 (ALM 89B), which is seen passing through Trafalgar Square on 25 August 2017.

Sullivan Buses took over operation of TfL route 217 from Metroline in June 2017. Depicting the new order were the attractive Enviro 400 MMC buses, as seen by Sullivan Buses E74 (JS17 SUL) passing Trinity Avenue on the Great Cambridge Road in Enfield on 5 June 2017.

The so-called Borisbus, or, even worse, 'New Routemaster', replaced the ill-fated Bendybuses, but still suffered from high levels of fare evasion. In this view we see Metroline's LT18 (LTZ 1018) at Hampstead Heath on 28 June 2013, working route 24.

Digital destination displays are notoriously difficult to photograph, as seen here on Centrebus YR59 NNT arriving at Waltham Cross on 19 February 2011. This Wright-bodied Scania was purchased new by this operator in December 2009.

The main railway line between Norwich and London, Liverpool Street, was closed for a number of weeks during the summer of 2004 between Ipswich and Manningtree to allow the track to be lowered inside the tunnel to accommodate higher freight trains. A variety of buses were used on an extensive shuttle between Ipswich and Manningtree. Here, First's H140 FLX leaves Ipswich railway station on 7 August 2004. This Northern Counties-bodied Leyland Olympian had been new to London Buslines in November 1990.

First Eastern Counties K740 JAH is a Northern Counties-bodied Dennis Lance that was purchased new in February 1993. In this 1999 view she is seen pulling out of the Turban Centre in Woodbridge, working route 83 to Bawdsey while in the care of a driver from the Saxmundham out-station.

Alexander-bodied Leyland Olympian G51 XLO was new to London Buslines in August 1989, but was working for First Blue Bus in Great Yarmouth when photographed passing through the bus station in the town in the summer of 2000.

The late 1980s and into the '90s saw a host of second-hand buses come to work in London as various companies sought to keep their operating costs down in order to win routes placed out for tender by London Regional Transport. Grey-Green's 491 (GND 491N), a Daimler Fleetline that was new to Greater Manchester PTE in October 1974, is seen at Cockfosters in 1991.

In December 1981, London Transport received the delivery of KYV 723X, an MCW Metrobus that is seen here in 1991 passing through Enfield Town and carrying the Leaside subsidiary name. Upon privatisation this was to become Cowie Leaside, and then later Arriva, as we know them today.

Many Leyland Nationals saw extended lives, having been re-bodied by East Lance and named the 'National Greenway'. Seen in Colchester in 2000 is Arriva's NIW 6512, which started life out as Crosville Leyland National FCA 6X before being re-bodied as a Greenway in 1993 and working for London & Country.

CT Plus 2524 (SN66 WRJ) is an Enviro 400H City, and was part of a batch acquired to work route 26 between Hackney Wick and Waterloo. She is seen here arriving at her destination on 27 August 2017.

Dennis Dart SLF KE03 TWA was new to Universitybus of Hatfield, trading as UNO, in April 2003. She is seen here leaving Potters Bar station on 1 November 2010, working service 810 through to Enfield Town.

Many of the so-called 'New Routemasters' operate in over-all advertising liveries that are changed regularly. Here we see Metroline's LT10 (LTZ 1010) passing through Trafalgar Square on 19 November 2016, working route 24.

Back in 2003, when this photograph was taken, First Capital were operating route W8 between Chase Farm Hospital and Picketts Lock, the latter of which is now known as the Lee Valley Centre. Here we see R426 SOY, a Dennis Arrow that was new in November 1997, passing through Enfield on 3 May 2003.

First Eastern Counties Alexander Dash-bodied Volvo B6 had been new to Kelvin Central in March 1994. A batch of these moved within First Group to East Anglia and they entered service here still in their former owner's livery. L103 WYS poses for the camera in Hoxne on the lovely 82 service that operated a four-hour round trip between Ipswich and Diss, taking in some beautiful Suffolk countryside.

Badgerline's L225 AAB is a Plaxton Verde-bodied Dennis Lance that was new to Midland Red West in May 1994. She is seen here leaving Bath, bound for Frome on 22 March 2003.

RM1650 (650 DYE) had been renumbered SRM3 when photographed close to Trafalgar Square on 14 July 2007 while working heritage route 9, having been repainted in to the Queens Silver Jubilee livery that was used in 1977. Heritage route 9 was introduced on 12 December 2005, running between Aldwych and Kensington, so that Routemaster buses could be retained after their withdrawal from normal service routes. The heritage version of route 9 was withdrawn on 25 July 2014.

Following privatisation in London, the London Buses operating subsidiary was bought by MTL, and in turn saw a few strange vehicle movements. One such arrival for use on non-London work was this Optare-bodied DAF, F848 YJX, which is seen in 1996 heading out of Enfield bound for Harlow on commercial route 310B. This bus was delivered new to Ogden of Haydock in 1989.

ECW-bodied Leyland Atlantean MEV 85V was delivered new to Colchester Borough Transport in December 1979. Carrying fleet number 85, she was captured by the camera entering the bus station in the town in 1996.

Wright-bodied Scania N632 XBU was purchased new in December 1995 by Bullock of Cheadle, but by the year 2000 she had migrated to Hadleigh in Suffolk to work for Beestons, a long-established independent in the area. She is seen here in the Old Cattle Market bus station in Ipswich having working in from Sudbury on a journey on route 91.

Carrying both Roadrunner and Townlink logos, this Plaxton-bodied Volvo B7TL was new to London United in April 2000. She is seen here at Waltham Cross on 25 November 2010, working service R3.

In October 2003 a batch of Transbus-bodied Volvo B7TLs came to First Eastern Counties at Ipswich for use on the successful Superoute 66 – the operation of which over the previous years had grown from Dennis Darts to full-length Scania L94s before requiring the use of double-deckers. Here AU53 HKL passes through Martlesham Heath village on 2 April 2005.

Back in 2005/6 I was working for Carters of Capel St Mary in Suffolk, and we had a nice school journey into Essex. ECW-bodied Leyland Olympian C664 LJR was new to Northern General in October 1985 and is photographed twenty years later close to Horsley Cross before working the school journey back in to Manningtree.

A surprising, but short-lived, addition to First Eastern Counties Ipswich depot in 1999 were a pair of Leyland Lynx buses. D876 ELL was originally delivered new to Merthyr Tydfil as D111 NDW in July 1987, but moved on two years later to the London Borough of Hillingdon, and was registered as 811 DYE a few months later in 1990. Bought by London Buses in 1991, she became part of the First CentreWest fleet upon privatisation, which enabled her transfer within First Group to Ipswich. Only one of the pair operated in service at Ipswich, and she was allocated to the small out-station at Sudbury, in whose care she was when photographed at East Bergholt High School.

First VSH69934 (BJ63 UJZ), a Volvo Hybrid with thirty-seven seats, arrives at Heathrow Central bus station on 4 March 2017.

J810 KHD is an Ikarus-bodied DAF that was new to London Buses in January 1992. On 30 June 2005 she was photographed in Norwich, heading for North Walsham while working for Sanders of Holt.

In 2014 a new Park and Ride service from Poppleton Bar to York city centre started, worked by First York Optare Versa V1110 EV buses. They are 11.1 metres long, with thirty-six seats, and are powered solely by electricity. Batteries are charged up overnight in the First York depot. During the day batteries can be topped up while the Optare Versas are on layover at Poppleton Bar, as shown by First York 49902 (YJ14 BHD) on 5 November 2014. (Robert Appleton)

On 22 February 1988 operation of route 313 passed to Grey-Green from London Country and was operated from their depot at Barking. Leyland Lynx E889 KYW is seen in Enfield Town in 1995.

New to London Buses in April 1992, Plaxton-bodied Dennis Dart J105 DUV was working for Regal Busways when photographed in Chelmsford on 12 May 2008, heading for Southend.

Cuffley station is the location for this view of Trustline's Marshall-bodied Dennis Dart R711 MEW, which is seen working local service C1 to Cheshunt on 5 July 2008. This bus had been new to London Northern in February 1998.

New to London Buslines in August 1989 was G50 XLO, an Alexander-bodied Leyland Olympian, which is seen here in the town centre of Slough in 1993 while working London Transport service 81 back to Hounslow.

Wright-bodied Scania S572 TPW was part of a batch delivered to First Eastern Counties' Ipswich depot in February 1999 for use on the Felixstowe group of services. In this 2001 view she is seen on the edge of Clopton in Suffolk, having worked a school service from Saxmundham to Wickham before running dead to this location. Here I was waiting before heading to the nearby Otley College to work service 68 back in to Ipswich.

Bristol VR YNW 401S was new to West Riding in March 1978 and remained in the fleet until March 1992 before being sold to Southend Transport. She was sold to New Enterprise of Tonbridge in August 1996 and was scrapped early in 1991. She is seen here in the smart livery of Southend Transport. (Peter Horrex collection)

Back in the days when you could still drive through the centre of Waltham Cross, Arriva Lea Valley J927 CYL, an Ikarus-bodied DAF SB220, is seen in 2000 collecting passengers for Hertford while working route 310a, the bus being new to the Cowie group in March 1992.

One of the first operators of low-floor wheelchair-accessible single-deckers in Greater Manchester was R. Bullock & Co. (Transport) Ltd of Cheadle. New in 1996, N630 XBU was a Scania L113CRL with a Wright Axcess-Ultralow forty-two seat body. She was photographed in Stockport bus station on 22 April 1996. (Robert Appleton)

Alexander-bodied Volvo B6 L101 PWR was new to Yorkshire Rider in April 1994, but had migrated south to Eastern Counties when photographed at Woodbridge in Suffolk in 2000, where she is seen awaiting departure time on route 82 to Framlingham.

This East Lancs-bodied Volvo, M42 EPV, was new to Ipswich Buses in April 1995. On 28 August 2001 she waits her time in Tower Ramparts bus station before heading off on route 9 to the estates of Whitton and Castle Hill.

Plaxton-bodied Dennis Dart SLF P434 NEX was part of a batch delivered new to Eastern Counties in November 1996. Carrying fleet number 43434, she is seen entering Ipswich on 2 April 2005, working service 65 from the Woodbridge area of Suffolk.

Devoid of fleet names, as indeed all buses are in this fleet that work on TfL contracted services, Sullivan Buses' AE20 (DS66 SUL) passes through Enfield Town on 22 May 2017. For these buses, owner Dean Sullivan has chosen prefixes to the registration numbers that represent employees' initials or other points of interest in the area.

Grey-Green 887 (E887 KYW) is a Leyland Lynx that was new to Cowie group in October 1987, and is seen here five years later in Walthamstow in 1992 while working on London Transport service 20 to Debden.

Shown as being delivered new to Optare of Leeds in April 1991, this Optare-bodied MAN was working for Seamarks of Luton when photographed in St Albans in 1992.

In January 1979 Great Yarmouth Transport purchased ECW-bodied Bristol VR CVF 30T. By 1997 this operator was part of First Group, operating within Eastern Counties as Blue Bus, but this VR was still wearing her previous owner's livery when photographed passing through the bus station in the town centre of Great Yarmouth.

July 1989 and London Buses took delivery of a batch of nine Alexander-bodied Scania N113 buses for use on London Transport service 263 from Potters Bar garage. Over the years further Scanias came to PB, not only to supplement the original batch, but also for use on route X43. Here London Northern S6 (F426 GWG) has strayed onto route 242 at Waltham Abbey in 1992.

Sovereign Bus & Coach had taken over operations of Jubilee coaches, and with it came this Leyland Lynx, F359 JVS, which had been new to Jubilee in September 1988 and was photographed in St Albans four years later, in 1992.

New to Stagecoach Cambus in October 2005, this Alexander-bodied Dennis Trident was photographed in the centre of Cambridge in January 2009 while working on service 1 to Fulbourn.

Arriva F895 BKK, photographed in Southend-on-Sea on 10 June 2006, was new to Maidstone & District back in September 1988.

With company owner Viv Carter behind the wheel, Carters Dennis Dart SLF P693 RWU heads out of Ipswich on 12 August 2006. Carters was set up in 1985 and operated both commercial and county council tendered services in south Suffolk and north Essex before being sold to Ipswich Buses in 2016.

Eastern Counties Plaxton-bodied Dennis Dart SLF A002 ODN has arrived at her destination of Aldeburgh from Ipswich on 19 April 2005, working service 65, which came the 'scenic' way through Rendlesham, Blaxhall and Snape.

London's so-called 'New Routemaster' buses look better in a livery other than plain red, as depicted here by Go-Ahead's LT60 (LTZ 1060), seen at Charing Cross on 19 November 2014 while wearing this heritage livery.

In May 2008 Metroline purchased a batch of Enviro 200s for use on their commercial services 84 and 242, and, fitted with digital destination equipment, this prevented their use from TfL routes. On a sunny 2 June 2009, DEL855 (LK08 DWJ) departs Waltham Cross at the start of her journey back to Potters Bar, taking in Cheshunt, Goffs Oak, Cuffley and Northaw.

In 1999 the long-established independent operator A. Mayne & Son Ltd bought its first low-floor wheelchair-accessible double-deckers – five long-wheelbase Dennis Tridents with East Lancashire eighty-one-seat bodies. One of them, V125 DJA, was in Ashton-under-Lyne bus station on 7 April 2000. (Robert Appleton)

Leaside Buses, which we know today as Arriva London North, were operating this Plaxton-bodied Dennis Dart, N677 GUM, when photographed in Southbury Road, Enfield, working route 307 in 1996. This bus had been delivered new just a few months earlier, in November 1995.

Wright-bodied Dennis Dart SLF was delivered new to Guildford & West Surrey in January 1995, and was photographed some seven years later in 2002 when passing through Guildford wearing full Arriva colours.

On 2 January 2018 an array of Arriva London North buses await attention over the pits at Enfield bus garage. Nearest the camera is LK16 BXZ, an ADL E20 MMC with B24F bodywork that was purchased in June 2016 for use on TfL contracted service 377. An Enviro 400 stands next in line, and then a couple of the DAF DW class, with the furthest of the DWs being of the older type, DW139, in use as a driver training bus.

Over the past decade the Park and Ride services in Ipswich have bounced between Ipswich Buses and First (Eastern Counties). Back in 2003 First didn't get a look in on these services, and here an Ipswich Buses Dennis Dart SLF with East Lancs bodywork heads in towards Ipswich Town centre on the Martlesham service.

Older Dennis Tridents, and indeed Volvos, are rapidly declining in use in London. Here Metroline TA643 (LK05 GGA) stands at Finsbury Park on 24 January 2018, about to work a journey on route 210 to Brent Cross.

Solent Blue Line Leyland Olympian F709 SDL passes through Southampton in 2003. This bus had been delivered new to this operator's owner, Musterphantom, in May 1989.

Delivered new to Viscount in March 1998, Stagecoach Volvo Olympian R581 JVA is seen that same year in the bus station in Huntingdon, heading for Peterborough on service 351.

The history of Chambers of Bures in Suffolk dates back to 1877, but more recently, in 2012, the company was sold to the Go-Ahead group. Seen here in Sudbury in 2000 bound for Colchester is Leyland Olympian G864 XDX, which was purchased new by Chambers in November 1989.

Ensign bus V115 MEV, a Dennis Trident that was new to Stagecoach Selkent in November 1999, is seen passing through Oakwood station on rail replacement work in October 2010.

Not the most attractive of buses, a batch of East Lancs-bodied Volvo B10M were delivered new in October 1989 to London & Country for use on London Transport tendered services. Here London & Country G614 BPH heads away from Putney Heath towards Kingston in 1993.

Wright-bodied Scania L113 P549 RNG was part of a batch acquired by Eastern Counties in the summer of 1997 for the Superoute 88 group of services between Ipswich, Stowmarket and Bury St Edmunds. Accident repairs to the offside have removed part of the route branding, which is irrelevant in this photograph anyhow, as the bus has strayed on to route 83 and is seen in 1999 opposite Bawdsey Church, prior to turning around and heading back to Ipswich.

One reason that I dislike LED or digital destination displays is that they often do not come out well in photographs. Arriving at her destination of Ipswich on route 91 on 16 May 2006 from Sudbury is Beestons East Lancs-bodied Scania, YN03 DDA.

Leyland Lynx E371 YRO was purchased by Jubilee of Stevenage in October 1987, and subsequently passed to Sovereign when Jubilee was acquired by that company. She is seen here in the bus station in Stevenage when ten years old in 1997, working Hertfordshire County Council contracted services SB8 and SB9.

Dennis Dart SLF X96 LBJ was part of a batch purchased by Ipswich Buses in September 2000. On 19 August 2006 she was photographed passing through the Maidenhall area of the town, heading for Ipswich Hospital on service 5.

Galloway are a well-known Suffolk independent, working on local bus services as well as coaching. On 26 April 2006 YR02 ZYL arrives in Ipswich before heading back out to Claydon on route 110. This Scania L94 was new to Anglian in April 2002.

The Bristol RE as a type survived in the Badgerline fleet until 1995, though this particular example, GHY 134K, passed to Northern Bus in 1992 and was scrapped by them in 1995. She is seen here taking passengers on board in the bus station in Wells, before working service 126 to Weston-super-Mare. This is a Bristol RELH with ECW DP49F bodywork that was new to Bristol Omnibus in July 1972.

In 1974 the red and cream buses of Southport Corporation were absorbed by the Merseyside Passenger Transport Executive. Many years later Arriva Mersyside introduced a red and cream livery for Southport Park and Ride services, as seen on 2144 (CX08 DJU), an Alexander Dennis Enviro 200, in Lord Street, Southport, on 27 February 2013. (Robert Appleton)

For a short time I worked for independent operator TWH. On loan in June 2013 was this Dennis Dart in Proctors Holidays livery, which is seen here at Ockendon station while working Essex County Council route 269 between Grays and Brentwood.

New to London Transport in December 1981, this MCW Metrobus M725 (KYV 725X) was working for London Buses subsidiary London Northern when photographed in heavy snow in Colney Hatch Lane, Muswell Hill, in February 1991.

ECW-bodied Leyland Olympian MUH 283X had been new to National Welsh in March 1982. Twelve years later she was photographed in the Essex seaside town of Southend-on-Sea, working local service 29 to Eastwood.

Alexander-bodied Volvo Olympian S130 RLE was new to Metroline in September 1998. Many of these ended their days with Metroline, based at Potters Bar, for use on commercially operated services 84 and 242. On 3 June 2006 AV30 heads out of Potters Bar station, bound for New Barnet from St Albans.

Routemaster ALD 966B was new to London Transport in July 1964 as RM1966. Some thirty years later, in 1994, I photographed her working in Blackpool.

Wright Handybus Dennis Dart JDZ2 392 was new to London Buses in September 1991, becoming part of the First CentreWest fleet and subsequently moving within First Group to Eastern Counties. She is seen here in 2000 at Hadleigh in Suffolk before working back to Ipswich wearing the so-called, but short-lived, First Anglia livery.

TPD 121X is a Roe-bodied Leyland Olympian that was new to London Country in June 1982. Here she arrives in Ipswich in 2001 while working for Beestons of Hadleigh on their 91 service between Sudbury and Ipswich.

London Transport's RML2318 (CUV 318C) was new in November 1965, and was working for one of the Go-Ahead London companies when photographed at Victoria in 2000.

After the purchase of Blackburn Transport in 2007, the Transdev operations in that area were revised, and inter-urban Lancashire United services gained a new livery, which included the red rose of Lancashire. This is shown on Optare Tempo X1200 1308 (YJ60 KAU), which was new in 2010, and is seen leaving Bolton on 30 April 2011 while working service 225 to Darwen, Blackburn, and Clitheroe. Historically, this had once been a Ribble service. (Robert Appleton)

The two town services operated by First Eastern Counties in Ipswich were worked with a mix of Dennis Darts and Volvo B6 buses, though I often managed to swap mine for a Scania or even a Bristol VR when I worked the Sunday late shift on the town routes. Here Wright-bodied Scania L94 S569 TPW poses for the camera in the Greenwich area of Ipswich on 16 January 2005.

Optare-bodied DAF SB 220 was new to Ipswich Buses in May 1994. On 2 February 2005 she was photographed leaving the Old Cattle Market bus station in the town, bound for Kesgrave on route 34.

London Suburban Bus operated some bus routes in North London for a time, before they were bought out by MTL/London Northern. Here L216 TWM, a Northern Counties-bodied Volvo, collects passengers at Archway, bound for Moorgate on route 271.

London Buslines Leyland Lynx D755 DLO was new in July 1987 for use on London Transport tendered services. She is seen here in Slough on 22 May 1993, heading back to Hounslow on route 81.

Throughout the 1980s and well into the 1990s the Leyland Titan, along with the Metrobus, were the mainstay of London's driver-only double-deck bus operations. In snowy conditions in February 1991, London Northern's T616 (NUW 616Y) heads up Colney Hatch Lane in Muswell Hill, closely followed by T655 on a light run from Finchley garage to take up work on route W7 between Muswell Hill and Finsbury Park.

Dennis Dart P285 MLD was new to Metroline in August 1996, but ten years later was captured by the camera heading out of Martlesham in Suffolk on a Suffolk County Council sponsored service. The destination is unknown due to these awful LED screens.

This Dennis Dart SLF with UVG bodywork was new to Marchwood of Totton in August 1997. In this view taken in Ipswich in 2004 she was working for Galloway Travel of Mendlesham and is seen heading out of town (despite what the destination shows) on local service 110 to Claydon.

In the summer of 2003 Plaxton-bodied Dennis Dart SLF is seen working in Guildford on Park and Ride service 200. This bus was new in March 1999 to Arriva West Sussex.

Stagecoach Alexander-bodied Dennis Trident GX06 DXT heads out of Chichester bound for Brighton on 27 October 2007. New to Southdown in 2006, this bus carries H47/28F bodywork.

Leyland Lynx G326 NUM had been new to Yorkshire Woollen in April 1990, but had migrated to East Anglia when photographed, working for Hedingham at Colchester on 9 March 2006.

GTX 758W is an ECW-bodied Bristol LHS6L with DP27F bodywork that was new to National Welsh in December 1980. She was working for Carters Coach Services when photographed at Hadleigh in Suffolk in 1998.

New to London Buses in November 1986, ECW-bodied Leyland Olympian D201 FYM was acquired by Ipswich Buses in August 2005, and was photographed in Ipswich the following year. She is now in preservation with the Bromley bus preservation group, having been acquired by them in June 2011.

Capital Citybus brought a splash of colour to London with their bright yellow livery. Leyland-bodied Olympian J142 YRM was new in October 1991, and is seen here on 15 April 1993 at Tottenham Hale station, working on London Transport service 123 to Ilford.

Chambers purchased Northern Counties-bodied Volvo N952 KBJ new in November 1995, and she was less than one year old when photographed entering the bus station in Colchester in the summer of 1996, heading for Bury St Edmunds on service 753.

A pair of Leyland Olympians in the Southern Vectis fleet stand at Ryde on the Isle of Wight in the summer of 1993. RDL 688X carries ECW bodywork with H45/32F seating and was new in April 1982, whereas G719 WDL is a Leyland-bodied example with CH43/29F seating that was new in November 1989.

Armchair of Brentford took delivery of G365 YUR, an Alexander-bodied Leyland Olympian, for use on London Transport's tendered bus network in June 1990. She was photographed at Golders Green in 1993.

Working for First Blue Bus in Great Yarmouth in 2000 was Alexander-bodied Leyland Olympian G50 XLO, which had been new to London Buslines in August 1989.

Ipswich Buses have had a few Dennis Falcons in their fleet, some purchased new and some second-hand. East Lancs-bodied G121 VDX was delivered new to Ipswich in August 1989, and is seen here in the town eleven years later in the summer of 2000, heading towards the Castle Hill and Whitton areas of the town.

Optare-bodied DAF SB220 G252 EHD was new to Wall of Fallowfield in August 1989. She was part of the Beestons of Hadleigh fleet when photographed in Sudbury early in 2001, working service 91 to Ipswich.

New to Stansted Transit in July 2003, Transbus Dart SLF KV03 ZGR was still working for that company three years later when photographed in Braintree on 17 June 2006.

In June 1994 Ambassador Travel took delivery of L71 UNG, an Alexander-bodied Volvo B6 with B41F seating. Photographed in Ipswich in 2000, she was working for Mulleys of Ixworth on Suffolk County Council sponsored service 103.

Plaxton-bodied Dennis Dart K282 XJB was new to Q-Drive buses in March 1993. Trading as 'The Bee Line', she is seen here in Slough on 22 May 1993.

In 2000 Blazefield-owned Yorkshire Coastliner received a batch of seven Volvo Olympians, which were the last built for operators in the United Kingdom. They had Alexander Royale bodies, and were 10.3 metres long with seventy-two semi-coach seats. One of these, 436 (W436 CWX), was opposite York railway station on 21 August 2004, working service 843 from Scarborough to Leeds, when seen. (Robert Appleton)

Arriva ENX3 (LJ61 CKK) makes the tight turn to head out of Chase Farm Hospital on 21 March 2014, working route 313 to Potters Bar. This Enviro 200 was new in October 2011 as part of a small batch ordered to work this TfL contracted service.

In May 2008 Metroline purchased a batch of Enviro 200 buses with B37F seating for use on their commercial services in Hertfordshire – routes 84 and 242. On 24 May 2014 Metroline DEL856 (LK08 DWL) and DEL857 (LK08 DWM) pass through Potters Bar station.

Arriva ENX8 (LJ61 CHZ), another from the batch purchased for route 313, is seen in Chingford on 1 December 2017.

After a successful service life, some buses go on to work as driver training vehicles. One such bus, N286 DWY, an Optare-bodied MAN new to Stanwell Buses in August 1995, is seen here on 9 February 2011 on the Hertford Road in Enfield, working for Transdev.

On 12 October 2011 Sullivan Buses PO51 UML collects students for Chancellors School outside Metroline's Potters Bar garage on service 841. This East Lancs-bodied Dennis Trident was new to Blue Triangle in November 2001.

Pictured in Cambridge on 8 January 2009 working for Stagecoach on Park and Ride duties is AE07 KZC, which was new in August 2007 to Stagecoach Cambus.

Blue Triangle GYE 468W is an MCW-bodied Metrobus that was new to London Transport in November 1980. She is seen here at Archway in north London on 16 November 2006, working on rail replacement duties for the London Underground.

2 April 2010 and First London's LK04 HYN, a Wright-bodied Volvo B7TL that was new in March 2004, powers its way past Metroline's Dennis Trident LR02 BDF at Childs Hill.

In July 1997 Harris Bus of West Thurrock took delivery of P345 ROO, an East Lancs-bodied Volvo Olympian. On 8 January 2009 she was photographed in the centre of Cambridge, working for Go Whippet.

These were nice buses to drive. R699 MEW is a Marshall-bodied Dennis Dart SLF that was new to MTL London Northern in May 1998. In this view taken on 15 May 2007 she is seen on the stand at Highgate Woods, prior to heading back to Barnet on TfL service 234.

Badgerline 5545 (EWS7 53W) is seen in Bath on 25 June 1992. She was a Bristol VRT/SL3 with Eastern Coach Works seventy-four seat body and was new in 1981 to Bristol Omnibus Company. When new, she was fitted with a Leyland 0.680 engine instead of the more normal Gardner 6LXB engine. (Robert Appleton)

Buses of Somerset 62191 (OIG 1791), a Volvo B10BLE with Wright Renown forty-three seat body, was about to enter Taunton bus station on 26 June 2015. 62191 was new to First Manchester in 2000 and was originally registered X685 ADK. (Robert Appleton)

Stagecoach Ribble 2224 (P224 VCK) was a long-wheelbase Volvo Olympian with Northern Counties Palatine I body with eighty-two seats, and was new in 1996. On 8 June 1997 she was in Blackhorse Street, Bolton, waiting to return to Preston on service 125. (Robert Appleton)

Most Leyland Olympians supplied to National Bus Company subsidiaries had Eastern Coach Works bodies, but a minority had full-height bodies built by C. H. Roe of Leeds. One of these was 9506 (JHU 905X), which was new to Bristol Omnibus Company in 1982. Seen here in later life on 27 June 1992, 9506 had just left Marlborough Street bus station in Bristol. (Robert Appleton)

Badgerline 5714 (E217 BTA), a Volvo Citybus B10M-50 with Alexander RH body. With an underfloor horizontal Volvo engine, and a high but flat lower deck floor, 5714 had eighty-two semi-coach seats, thirty-five of them on the lower deck. E217 BTA was new to Western National in 1988, and transferred to Badgerline in 1989. She was photographed leaving Bath for Bristol on 25 June 1992. (Robert Appleton)

Stagecoach Ribble Buses 1478 (TRN 478V) was a Leyland Atlantean AN68A/1R with Eastern Coach Works seventy-four seat body that was new to Ribble in 1980. Photographed in Lord Street, Southport, on 12 August 1995, she was working service 102 from Preston. (Robert Appleton)

With the advent of low-floor wheelchair-accessible single-deckers, Stagecoach Group bought a large number of MAN 18.220 buses with Alexander ALX300 forty-two seat bodies. Stagecoach Manchester 105 (S10 5TRJ) was new in December 1998. On 21 August 1999 she was working in Cheadle Hulme, near Stockport. (Robert Appleton)

In 2014 First Group operations in the Taunton and Bridgwater areas of Somerset were rebranded as Buses of Somerset with a new livery and the absence of First logos. At Taunton bus station on 26 June 2015 were two Volvo B6BLE buses with Wright Crusader thirty-eight seat bodies that were new to First York in 2002. 40582 (UHW 661) and 40584 (HIG 8790) were originally registered YJ51 RHZ and YJ51 RJU. (Robert Appleton)

Badgerline 108 (D108 GHY) was a Volvo B10M-61 with Alexander P fifty-three-seat body, and was new in 1987. She is seen at work in Weston-super-Mare on 22 June 1992. With the large badger emblem on the side, there is no doubt as to the ownership of this bus! (Robert Appleton)

Stagecoach Ribble 264 (L664 MSF) at Blackburn bus station on 5 July 1995. L664 MSF was a Volvo B6 with Alexander Dash forty-seat body and was new to Stagecoach Fife Scottish in 1993. She was transferred to Stagecoach Ribble in 1994. (Robert Appleton)

First Huddersfield 4054 (N454 JUG), a Dennis Lance with Cummins rear engine and an 11-metre-long Plaxton Verde body, was new in 1995. She is seen leaving Huddersfield bus station on 12 February 1999. First Huddersfield was previously part of Yorkshire Rider Group, which was bought by the Badgerline Group in 1994. Several Badgerline Group companies bought the Dennis Lance in the period 1993 to 1995. (Robert Appleton)

Some buses have an extended life, going on to be used for other things than carrying passengers. Arriva's 'Bus 4 Life', R423 TJW, is a Plaxton-bodied Scania that was new to Midland Red North, and is seen here at Enfield bus garage on 12 May 2017.

In the summer of 2016 Arriva London North purchased a small batch of these E200MMCs for use on TfL route 377, which runs between Ponders End and Oakwood, taking in some narrow residential streets. Here Arriva EN35 (LK16 BXX) passes through Enfield on 23 May 2017.

Keighley & District H516 RWX is a Northern Counties-bodied Leyland Olympian that was new in August 1990. She was photographed in May 1991 collecting passengers in Keighley while working service 712 to Silsden.

United's GUP 908N is an ECW-bodied Bristol LH6L that was new to this operator in February 1975. In this May 1991 view, she is seen in Ripon. United took over 200 of the Bristol LH new, as well as some second-hand examples.